ATAMANSHA

The Story of Maria Nikiforova, the Anarchist Joan of Arc

by Malcolm Archibald

BLACK CAT PRESS
Edmonton, Alberta

First published 2007
Copyright © 2007 Black Cat Press

Library and Archives Canada Cataloguing in Publication:

*Atamansha : the Story of Maria Nikiforova, the Anarchist Joan
of Arc* by Malcolm Archibald.

ISBN 978-0-9737827-0-7

1. Nikiforova, Marusia, 1885-1919.
2. Anarchists–Ukraine–Biography.
3. Revolutionaries–Ukraine–Biography.
4. Ukraine–History–Revolution, 1917-1921.
5. Soviet Union–History–Revolution, 1917-1921.

DK265.8.U4 A78 2007   947.7/0841 22   C2007-906923-1

BLACK CAT PRESS
4508 118 Avenue
Edmonton, Alberta
Canada T5W 1A9
www.blackcatpress.ca

Contents

Introduction

The Ukrainian anarchist Maria Nikiforova (1887–1919) has sometimes been compared to Joan of Arc. Like Joan she started from humble origins and, improbably, became a ferocious military commander who was captured and executed by her sworn enemies. And, like Joan, she was a fanatic who pursued her goals in a violent, ruthless fashion.

But there is no cult of Maria Nikiforova. There are no shelves of books devoted to her life in any language. Although she played a prominent role in the Russian Revolutions of 1917 and the subsequent Civil War, she was virtually expunged from Soviet histories of the period. A biographical dictionary of the Russian Revolution published in the Soviet Union which includes hundreds of names does not mention her, indeed mentions only a couple of dozen women. There are entries on the Bolshevik heroines Alexandra Kollontai, Larissa Reissner, and Inessa Armand but none of these women held independent military commands like Nikiforova.

There is no scholarly biography of Maria Nikiforova, no historiography of her life which only needs to be updated and possibly reinterpreted. Partly this is because she spent most of her life in the underground: she joined an anarchist terrorist group at age 16 and was really only "above ground" for two years (1917-1919). So there are very few documents to trace her activities and almost no photos. Recognition can be fatal for a terrorist and so it was for Nikiforova in the end. Such accounts of her life which exist are usually found in memoir literature or fiction. Most of these accounts are hostile to Nikiforova and tend to depict her as repulsive and evil.

Nikiforova was a Ukrainian and her activities in the

Russian Revolution and Civil War took place mostly in Ukraine[1] but she has been largely ignored by Ukrainian historians. She was anti-nationalist and, like the Ukrainian anarchist movement in general, she couldn't be assimilated to a nationalist historical perspective.

Even writers sympathetic to anarchism have, as a rule, neglected her. Although she was closely associated with the famous peasant anarchist Nestor Makhno, books about Makhno scarcely mention her. And yet in 1918 Nikiforova was already famous as an anarchist atamansha (military leader) throughout Ukraine, while Makhno was still a rather obscure figure operating in a provincial backwater. She is absent from the works of Peter Arshinov, Voline, and Paul Avrich[2]. Alexandre Skirda's book on Makhno mentions her but only devotes one paragraph to her in a work of 400 pages.[3] Exceptions to the rule are Makhno himself and his former adjutant Victor Belash. In his memoirs (which only cover 22 months of revolution and civil war) Makhno provides eye-witness accounts of a number of dramatic incidents in which Nikiforova played a leading role. Belash, whose work was rescued from the files of the Soviet secret police, also presents primary source material about her.

Since the collapse of the Soviet Union there has been tremendous interest in Russia and Ukraine in filling in the "white patches" in their history. Makhno and Nikiforova have benefited from this interest with many books on Makhno being published and a few essays on Nikiforova. The archives have yielded some solid information;

---

1 Under the Russian Empire which ended in 1917 Ukraine was not a political entity but a collection of provinces often referred to as "South Russia" or "Little Russia".

2 Arshinov, P., *History of the Makhnovist Movement 1918-1921* (London, 2006); Voline, *The Unknown Revolution* (Montréal, 2004); Avrich, P., *The Russian Anarchists* (Oakland, 2005).

3 Skirda, A., *Anarchy's Cossack* (Oakland, 2004). This book was first published in France in 1982. Skirda's English translator confuses Nikiforova with a Bolshevik commissar.

for example, Nikiforova's service record exists since she was once a member of the Red Army. Gradually a clearer picture of her life is coming to light and it is possible to establish a reasonably reliable narrative although many ambiguities remain.

The following sketch of Nikiforova's life is based mainly on secondary sources published in Russian and Ukrainian in the last two decades.

The Young Terrorist

According to tradition, Maria Grigorevna Nikiforova was born in the Ukrainian city of Alexandrovsk[4] in 1885, the daughter of an officer who had been a hero of the last Russo-Turkish War. Although this story might help to explain her later martial ardour, it seems unlikely. For even the daughter of an impoverished officer would be unlikely to leave home at 16 to earn a living on our own as Maria did.

At the turn of the 19th century, Alexandrovsk was a rapidly industrializing city with a large and militant working class population. Under the conditions of the time there was little paid work for women, but Maria was able to find employment as a baby sitter, sales clerk and, finally, a bottle washer in a vodka distillery.

Around the same time she became a factory worker, Nikiforova also joined a local group of anarcho-communists. This political tendency was distinguished from other left-wing groups, including other anarchists, by the belief that human society had already reached a level that could allow an immediate transition to communism. Anarcho-communist organizers first appeared in Ukraine in 1903

---

4 Today Zaporizhzhia.

and enjoyed considerable success among the working class youth of industrial centres. During the revolutionary events of 1905-07 there were as many as 90 anarcho-communist groups in Ukraine, more numerous and better-organized than their counterparts in Russia.

Many of these groups, including the one Maria belonged to, espoused motiveless terror (*bezmotivny terror*) which advocated the necessity of attacking agents of economic repression based solely on the class position they occupied. This economic terrorism was a change from earlier varieties of Russian terrorism in which the targets of the terrorists were political tyrants. After serving some kind of probation, Maria became a full-fledged militant (*boevik*), empowered to take part in expropriations (to raise money for the cause) and terrorist acts.

Our age has also not lacked "motiveless terror" but it is important to try to see the Ukrainian anarchist terrorists in the context of their own times, not ours. The early years of the 20th century created pent-up frustrations among the lower classes of the Russian Empire because of the failure of revolutionary activity to change the country's socio-political order in any meaningful way. This was an empire headed by a monarch who was an honorary member of the "Union of the Russian People", an organization roughly equivalent to the Klu Klux Klan. Under prevailing conditions it was not just the anarchists who resorted to terror against the regime. All the socialist groups used terror. In fact, even middle class liberals endorsed the use of terror against tsarist repression. And although the Russian anarchists never numbered more than a few thousand, the ranks of their sympathizers were many times larger.

Maria participated in a bomb attack on a passenger train. No one was hurt but some wealthy passengers were terrified. Another bomb killed a plant manager, causing the plant to shut down for an extended period. An attack on the business office of an agricultural machine plant in Alexandrovsk resulted in the chief cashier and a guard being killed and 17,000 rubles stolen. When the police finally closed in, Maria tried to kill herself with a bomb, but it didn't explode and she ended up in prison.

At her trial in 1908 she was accused of the murder of a policeman and taking part in armed robberies at four different locations. The court sentenced the young anarchist to death but later, because of her age (in the Russian Empire adulthood began at 21), the sentence was commuted to 20 years at hard labour. She was transferred, first to Petro-Pavlovsk Fortress in the Russian capital and then conveyed to Siberia to serve her sentence.

It's hard to determine exactly when, but at some point in her life Maria Nikiforova began to be known as "Marusya", one of the many Slavic diminutives for "Maria". In folklore she is always referred to as Marusya and she certainly tolerated the name herself, allowing even strangers to address her as Marusya. Therefore we shall use it here.

The Grand Tour

Marusya didn't spend long in Siberia. According to one version, she organized a riot in the Narymsk prison and escaped through the taiga to the Great Siberian Railway. Eventually she reached Vladivostok, and then Japan. There she was helped by Chinese student-anarchists who bought her a ticket to the U.S. She found a temporary home among the large group of anarchist-emigrants from the Russian Empire, mainly of Jewish origin, who had settled in New York and Chicago. Apparently Marusya published propaganda articles in the anarchist Russian language press under various pseudonyms.

Around 1912 Marusya returned to Europe, settling in Paris. In 1913 she paid a visit to Spain where she was able to share her knowledge of "actions" with the Spanish anarchists. While taking part in an anarchist bank robbery in Barcelona, Marusya was wounded and had to undergo treatment secretly at a clinic in France.

In the autumn of 1913 she turned up in Paris again, hanging around the cafes and meeting poets and artists as well as the various Russian politicos, including the Social Democrat Vladimir Antonov-Ovseyenko who was later to help her out of some sticky situations. She discovered in herself a talent, or at least a predilection, for painting and sculpture and attended a school for artists.

Marusya also acquired a husband, the Polish anarchist Witold Bzhostek. This was surely some sort of marriage of convenience for the couple spent long periods apart and Marusya continued to use her own surname. Nevertheless they seemed devoted to each other and ultimately shared the same fate.

At the end of 1913, Marusya attended a conference of Russian anarcho-communists held in London. She was one of 26 delegates and signed the registration sheet as "Marusya". One of the main concerns of this conference was the lack of anarchist educational and agitational tracts, especially in comparison with their Marxist competitors.

This almost idyllic life came to an abrupt end with World War I. The war split the left-wing groups into pro-war and anti-war factions. The anarchists were no exception with the anarcho-communists close to Kropotkin taking an anti-German position. Marusya seems to have sided with Kropotkin and not just in theory for she enrolled in a French military school and graduated with the rank of an officer. According to her own story, she was eventually posted to the Salonika theatre of the war and was there when revolution broke out in Russia.

Like many left-wing Russian emigrants, Marusya made her way back to Russia in 1917. Reaching Petrograd, she immediately threw herself into revolutionary activity.

Revolutionary Days in Petrograd

Petrograd was the seat of two competing organs of power – the Provisional Government and the Petrograd Soviet. The Provisional Government, lacking in legitimacy since it had never been properly elected, was run by liberal and right-wing socialist politicians. Unwilling and unable to end Russia's participation in the World War and solve the land question in the countryside, the Provisional Government lurched from one crisis to the next. The Petrograd Soviet included more radical groups such as the Bolsheviks who were determined not to stop with destroying the tsarist system but to finish off the bourgeois order as well.

The Russian anarchists, as was often the case in 1917-18, acted as shock troops for the better-organized groups on the extreme left. The revolutionary activities of the anarchists brought down repression from the Provisional Government which arrested 60 of them in June, 1917, in Petrograd. One of those remaining in freedom was the anarcho-communist I. S. Bleikhman, a popular deputy of the Petrograd Soviet. Bleikhman planned a huge anti-government demonstration for July 3[5] which would involve military personnel as well as militant workers. The participation of sailors from the nearby Kronstadt naval base was crucial and the anarchists put together a team of agitators to persuade the sailors to take part.

---

5 Dates in Russia in 1917 were 13 days behind Western calendars. The Russian calendar was synchronized with the rest of the world in February 1918.

Having recently arrived in Russia, Marusya was one of the anarchists who went to Kronstadt. She gave a series of speeches on the huge Anchor Square to crowds as large as 8,000 to 10,000 sailors, urging them not to stand aside from their brothers in the capital. Partly thanks to her efforts many thousands of sailors went to Petrograd to march in the demonstrations of July 3 and 4 which almost toppled the Provisional Government. Although some Bolshevik organizations supported the demonstrations, that Party's leadership rejected the uprising as "premature", dooming it to failure.

The government began hunting down the Bolsheviks and anarchists. Some of the Bolsheviks, including Marusya's friend Alexandra Kollontai, ended up in prison while others escaped to nearby Finland. Bleikhman was given sanctuary by the Kronstadt sailors who protected him from arrest. Marusya decided it was a good time to return to Ukraine and help revive the anarchist movement there. In July 1917 she arrived back in Alexandrovsk, after an eight-year odyssey which had taken her around the world.

Marusya – the Person and the Activist

At this point in her biography it seems appropriate to take up the perplexing question of Marusya's sexuality. According to some published sources, admittedly written after her death by people who were hostile to her, Marusya was what would now be called an "intersex" person. This view is reflected in several physical descriptions, for example the former Makhnovist Chudnov writes of meeting her in 1918: "This was a woman of 32 – 35, medium height, with an emaciated, prematurely aged face in which there was something of a eunuch or hermaphrodite. Her hair was cropped short in a circle."

The Bolshevik agitator Kiselev writes in his memoirs about meeting her in 1919: "Around 30 years old. Thin with an emaciated face, she produced the impression of an old maid type. Narrow nose. Sunken cheeks. She wore a blouse and skirt and a small revolver hung from her belt." Kiselev goes on to accuse her of being a cocaine addict. Most of the Bolshevik descriptions of Marusya are at this level.

An exception is the Bolshevik Raksha who met Marusya in the spring of 1918:

"I had heard that she was a beautiful woman... Marusya was sitting at a table and had a cigarette in her teeth. This she-devil really was a beauty: about 30, gypsy-type with black hair and a magnificent bosom which filled out her military tunic."

Another description from the summer of 1918:

"A carriage flew down the street at a mad speed. Carelessly sprawled in it was a young brunette wearing a kubanka[6] at a rakish angle. Standing on the footboard was a broad-shouldered chap wearing red cavalry britches. The brunette and her bodyguard had all sorts of weapons hanging from them."

Generally the physical descriptions fall into these two camps, one emphasizing attractiveness, the other repulsiveness. One suspects the Bolshevik memoirists, finding her ideology unattractive, tried to make her external appearance ugly as well. What we do know for certain is that Marusya was a charismatic individual who made a strong impression on people she met and was capable of influencing them purely on the strength of her personality. Her comrades-in-arms were fiercely loyal to her and she

6 Kubanka: Cossack fleece hat.

returned their loyalty in kind.

Marusya's political views are well known from her numerous speeches. Prison, hard labour, and her global wanderings only strengthened the convictions of her youth. She frequently said: "The anarchists are not promising anything to anyone. The anarchists only want people to be conscious of their own situation and seize freedom for themselves." Her credo, which she expressed over and over again, was that "The workers and peasants must, as quickly as possible, seize everything that was created by them over many centuries and use it for their own interests."

On a tactical level, Marusya was influenced by the veteran anarchist Apollon Karelin whom she met in Petrograd. Karelin represented a tendency known as "Soviet anarchism" which encouraged anarchists to participate in Soviet institutions so long as they were acting to push the Revolution along in the right direction – the direction of more freedom. As soon as the Soviets began to deviate from this path, the anarchists were to rebel against them. Karelin himself became a member of the highest organ of Soviet power in 1918. Many anarchists disapproved of this tactic, especially since they were usually a distinct minority in the organs of Soviet power.

Alexandrovsk & Gulai-Polye

Arriving in Alexandrovsk, Marusya found a local Anarchist Federation had been set up with about 300 members but not much influence on local events. Marusya shook things up – she had an instant following among the factory workers and carried out the successful expropriation of one million rubles from the Badovsky distillery (possibly the one where she had worked). Part of the money was donated to the Alexandrovsk Soviet.

Alexandrovsk happened to be the capital of the uyezd[7] in which Gulai-Polye was situated. This "village" of 17,000 was the home of Nestor Makhno, the leading figure of the local Anarcho-Communist Group which had a membership in the hundreds. Makhno maintained close relations with the Alexandrovsk Anarchist Federation, visiting it frequently although he was skeptical of its activities (or lack thereof). The Alexandrovsk anarchists were also critical of

Makhno

Makhno, accusing him of leading a political party striving to seize power.

Marusya took it upon herself to travel to Gulai-Polye (about 80 km. east of Alexandrovsk but much farther by train) to straighten out the local anarchists who were not squeezing the bourgeoisie hard enough in her opinion. On August 29, 1917 she addressed a well-attended open-air meeting, chaired by Makhno, in the village's public garden.

Marusya preached the gospel of insurrection – rebel, rebel until all organs of power are eliminated. Carry the Revolution through to the end now, she said, or Capital will revive. Immediate action was also called for because of the assault on the Revolution by state power in Ukraine connected with the appearance of the government of the Central Rada[8]. Not beating around the bush, Marusya

---

7 Uyezd – an administrative subdivision of a province. Alexandrovsk Uyezd was part of Yekaterinoslav Province and included several raions, one of which was Gulai-Polye Raion.

8 The Central Rada was a Ukrainian nationalist government based in Kiev which

called for terrorist action against supporters of the fledgling Ukrainian state.

While Marusya was haranguing the locals, Makhno was suddenly handed two telegrams. Interrupting Marusya, he told the stunned audience "The Revolution is in danger!" Both telegrams were from Petrograd – one from the Provisional Government, the other from the Petrograd Soviet. Both told of General Kornilov's mutiny and his advance on Petrograd to put an end to the Revolution. The Soviet's telegram suggested forming local "Committees for the Salvation of the Revolution".

As the crowd buzzed a voice rang out: "Our brothers' blood is already flowing but here the counter-revolutionaries are walking around laughing." The speaker pointed to a certain Ivanov, a former secret policeman. Marusya immediately jumped down from the platform and "arrested" Ivanov who was now surrounded by an angry mob. But Makhno intervened to save the life of the former cop whom he described as "harmless".

The Gulai-Polye Peasant Union and the Anarcho-Communist Group followed the advice of the Petrograd Soviet with a slight change: they formed a Committee for the *Defense* of the Revolution. Its first activity was confiscating all the weapons in the hands of the local bourgeoisie. Marusya had something slightly different in mind. In the nearby town of Orekhov were stationed two regiments of the regular army. Marusya proposed to seize their weapons.

She organized a group of about 200 militants and on September 10 they travelled to Orekhov by train. They were poorly armed having only a couple dozen rifles and a simi-

---

was formed in the spring of 1917 and which had an uneasy relationship with the Russian Provisional Government based in Petrograd. "Rada" is the Ukrainian word for "Soviet".

lar number of revolvers confiscated from the Gulai-Polye police station. Arriving in Orekhov, they surrounded the headquarters of the regiments. The commander succeeded in escaping but some of the junior officers were captured. Marusya dispatched them with her own hand, showing her willingness to kill anyone who belonged to the despised "officers' caste". The rank-in-file soldiers were only too glad to turn in their arms and disperse to their homes.The weapons were taken to Gulai-Polye and Marusya returned to Alexandrovsk.

The organs of the Provisional Government in Alexandrovsk were headed by a chief commissar B. Mikhno (a liberal) and a military commissar S. Popov (an SR)[9]. These authorities were disturbed about the goings-on in Gulai-Polye, in particular, the confiscation of weapons from the property-owning class and the dividing up of large estates among the peasants. The local organs in Gulai-Polye, thoroughly infiltrated by the anarchists, began to receive threatening orders from the higher authorities.

These orders were ignored in Gulai-Polye; in fact, Makhno took the offensive by travelling to Alexandrovsk with another delegate, B. Antonov, to meet directly with workers' groups. The two anarchists were shown around the city by Marusya who took them to a number of workplace meetings. Since Makhno and Antonov had mandates from the Gulai-Polye Soviet, the authorities didn't dare touch them. With Marusya it was a different story, and after Makhno and Antonov had left the city she was arrested at her apartment and taken to prison by car.

Matters soon took an unpleasant turn for the authorities.

9 SR: member of the Party of Socialist-Revolutionaries, a left-wing but non-Marxist political party which claimed to represent the peasantry. In 1917 it was the largest socialist party in Russia but was prone to factionalism. The left-wing of the party split off to form a separate party – the Left-SRs. The Party also had nationalist variants, especially in Ukraine.

Marusya enjoyed great popularity among the workers of Alexandrovsk and news of her arrest spread like
wildfire. On the morning after her arrest a delegation of
workers visited the commissars to demand her release.
Their demand was refused. But there was also a Soviet in
Alexandrovsk which shared power with the official government. A procession of workers was organized which
marched to the Soviet to demand justice. Plants sat idle
with their sirens wailing while the march took place. On
the way the demonstrators encountered the chairman of
the Soviet, Mochalov (a Menshevik[10]), who was literally
forced into a horse-drawn cab with some worker delegates
and dispatched to the prison. Marusya was released and
brought back to the demonstration where she was passed
over the heads of the workers to the front of the crowd
massed outside the building of the Soviet. Marusya, who
possessed a powerful voice used the occasion to make a
stirring speech calling for the workers to struggle against
the Government and for a society free of all authority.

Meanwhile news of Marusya's arrest was causing havoc
in Gulai-Polye. Makhno managed to reach Commissar
Mikhno by telephone; threats were exchanged and Mikhno
hung up. The anarchists loaded up a train with militants
and set out to attack the government in Alexandrovsk. En
route they received news of Marusya's release and held a
celebration instead.

One practical result of all this was new elections to the
Alexandrovsk Soviet which produced a more left-wing
body, including some anarchists, which was prepared to
tolerate the revolutionary activities in Gulai-Polye.

---

10 Menshevik: in 1903 the Russian Social Democratic Labour Party split into two
factions which later crystallized into two separate parties: the Mensheviks (moderate
socialists) and the Bolsheviks (revolutionary socialists).

The October Revolution in Ukraine

Like most anarchists, Marusya received news of the October Revolution with enthusiasm. The anarchists regarded the coup by the Bolsheviks and the Left SRs (forming the so-called Left Bloc) as a further stage in the withering away of the State. Following the demise of tsardom and the bourgeois state, they thought the Left Bloc government was a temporary phenomenon which would soon disappear.

Marusya spent the fall organizing "Black Guard" detachments in Alexandrovsk and Yelizavetgrad[11], a central Ukrainian city, which also had a strong anarchist federation. According to one historian, Marusya was responsible for the murder of the chairman of the Yelizavetgrad Soviet.

After the October Revolution, the soviets in many Ukrainian cities oriented themselves towards the Ukrainian Central Rada in Kiev rather than the Soviet government in Petrograd. In Alexandrovsk the decision was made on November 22, 1917 and the vote was 147 to 95 in favour of becoming part of the Kiev-based Ukrainian National Republic.

When the nationalist government in Kiev refused to rec ognize the Left Bloc government in Moscow, the Left Bloc invaded Ukraine with a motley force composed of various Red Guard units. Both sides engaged in an "echelon[12] war", advancing and retreating along the railway lines, much like the contemporaneous Mexican Revolution.

In December 1917 Marusya formed an alliance with the Bolshevik organization in Alexandrovsk with the aim of overthrowing the local Soviet. The Bolsheviks received a

---

11 Now Kirovohrad.
12 Echelon: a troop train.

secret shipment of arms while the
anarchists were able to arrange the
support of a detachment of sailors
from the Black Sea Fleet led by M.
V. Mokrousov[13]. On December
12, 1917, Mokrousov appeared at a
joint meeting of the Alexandrovsk
Soviet and factory committees and
demanded the Soviet be re-con-
stituted with members who were
Bolsheviks, Left SRs, or anarchists.
The members of other parties (Men-   Mokrousov
sheviks and SRs) fled the scene and the new Soviet took
over.

On December 25-26, 1917, Marusya's detachment went to
Kharkhov and helped the Left Bloc establish soviet power
in the city. Her troops engaged in an action there which
became her trademark – looting the shops and distributing their goods to the inhabitants. On December 28-29 her
Black Guards took part in battles with the haidamaks[14] at
Yekaterinoslav, successfully establishing Soviet power in
that city as well. According to her own version of events,
her detachment was the first to enter the city and she
personally disarmed 48 soldiers.

The Left Bloc dismissed the Russian Constituent Assembly[15] at the beginning of January, 1918, making Civil War
virtually inevitable. Lacking a strong base in the population, especially in the countryside, the Left Bloc needed

13 Aleksei Vasilyevich Mokrousov (1887-1959) was the only anarchist commander
who managed to survive not only the Civil War but Stalin's repressions. He fought in
the Spanish Civil War and also directed partisan groups in World War II.

14 Haidamak: the atavistic term the Central Rada used to refer to its troops. Haidamaks were Ukrainian rebels of the 18th century, fighting against Polish rule.

15 The Constituent Assembly was a parliamentary body elected in 1917 which only
held one session before being dismissed by the ruling Left Bloc, which had received
only a minority of the seats. By dismissing the Constitutent Assembly, the government
of Lenin made clear its refusal to relinquish power through democratic processes.

allies and only the anarchists shared their implacable hatred of the bourgeoisie. The Left Bloc sought help especially from the anarchists in Ukraine where there were a number of groups like Marusya's and Makhno's which had military capabilities.

Meanwhile in Alexandrovsk the new regime was under threat by troops of the Central Rada. The forces the Soviet was able to muster were not as numerous or as well armed as the haidmaks (who had armoured cars). The revolutionaries decided not to use Mokrousov's artillery in order to avoid destroying the city. After three days of street fighting, the Bolsheviks and anarchists were forced to withdraw. The balance shifted when Red Guards from Moscow and Petrograd arrived. On January 2, 1918, the haidamaks retreated to the right bank of the Dnieper and power in the city fell to the hands of the newly formed Revolutionary Committee (Revkom)[16]. On January 4 Nestor Makhno and his brother Savva showed up with an 800-strong Black Guard detachment from Gulai-Polye. Nestor was invited to join the Revkom and the Federation of Anarchists was allowed to appoint two delegates, one of whom was Marusya who became the deputy leader of the Revkom.

---

16 Revkom: Revolutionary Committee – after the October Revolution local Soviets set up Revolutionary Committees to organize the military defense of the Revolution.

The Cossack Threat

The haidamaks had retreated, but now a new danger was threatening the revolutionary city. A convoy of echelons loaded with Cossacks (and their horses) was approaching the city from the External Front[17] on their way to the Don to join the counter-revolutionary movement of the reactionary General Kaledin. Realizing the danger the Cossacks represented to the Revolution, the Alexandrovsk insurgents decided to stop them.

The anarchists led their detachments across the nearby Kichkass suspension bridge over the Dnieper and dug in along the railway tracks. Soon the Cossacks showed up. Contact was established by telephone and a meeting arranged between representatives of the two sides. Makhno and Marusya were part of the delegation which travelled by locomotive to the meeting point. The Cossack officers were in a belligerent mood and claimed they had 18 echelons of Cossacks and another seven echelons of haidamaks and no one was going to stop them. Negotiations were broken off.

The first Cossack train which tried to break through was met with heavy fire and started to back up suddenly, colliding with the train behind and causing a wreck with loss of life to both men and horses. Soon a new truce party of Cossacks arrived which capitulated to the Alexandrovsk Revkom. They gave up their weapons but insisted on keeping their horses and saddles for "cultural" reasons.

The disarming of the Cossacks was spread over many days and the local politicians took the opportunity to try to win them over to the Revolution. At one outdoor meeting thousands of Cossacks were addressed by a series of social-

---

17 External Front: the front against Russia's main enemies in World War I – Germany and Austro-Hungary. There were soon to be many internal fronts as well as the civil war spread.

ist orators, with little effect. The Cossacks stood around smoking, occasionally laughing at the speakers.

Then Marusya stepped to the podium and began to speak. Now the Cossacks were paying attention. "Cossacks, I must tell you that you are the butchers of the Russian workers. Will you continue to be so in the future, or will you acknowledge your own wickedness and join the ranks of the oppressed? Up to now you have shown no respect for the poor workers. For one of the tsar's rubles or a glass of wine, you have nailed them living to the cross."

As Marusya continued in this vein many of the Cossacks removed their caps and bowed their heads. Soon some of them were weeping like children.

A knot of Alexandrovsk intellectuals was standing in the crowd. They told each other: "The speeches of the Left Bloc representatives seem so pale in comparison with the speeches of the anarchists and, in particular, with the speech of M. Nikiforova." One upshot of the meetings, which went on for days, was that a number of Cossacks maintained contact with the Gulai-Polye anarchists even after they went home to the Kuban and other regions.

After the Cossacks had been disarmed, Marusya and Makhno returned to their duties on the Alexandrovsk Revkom. Makhno had been assigned the "dirty" job of heading a tribunal which passed sentence on various political prisoners collected by the new political order. Among the prisoners who came before him was Mikhno, the former Provisional Government commissar who had threatened him repeatedly and jailed Marusya. Makhno released him, saying he was an honest man who was only following orders.

Makhno was not inclined to be magnanimous with an-other prisoner, the former prosecutor Maksimov. When

Makhno was a prisoner in the Alexandrovsk prison many years earlier, Maksimov had made sure his stay was as unpleasant as possible. Considering the evidence against him, Makhno felt justified in sentencing Maksimov to be shot. But the other members of the Revkom, including Marusya, interceded on his behalf. Although they agreed he was a counter-revolutionary, their regime was too shaky to be executing someone who was well regarded in the city. Makhno didn't give in easily and it was only after an all-night meeting that he agreed to remand Maksimov for further review of his case.

Makhno was soon fed up with the Alexandrovsk Revkom (among other things, they wouldn't let him blow up the prison) and decided to return to Gulai-Polye with his detachment. The other members of the Revkom came to the train station to see them off – most went there by automobile, Marusya on horseback. At the station the detachment sang the anarchist battle hymn, then embarked.[18]

Marusya was able to hold her Black Guard detachment together and began to act as an independent military commander. It was at this point that Marusya became a player on the national stage rather than just a local figure.

---

18 The lyrics were sung to the tune of an old revolutionary song, *"Land and Freedom"* and were more or less as follows:

> *We sing our song under thunder and fury,*
> *Under exploding shells, under blazing fires,*
> *Under the black banner of titanic struggle,*
> *Under the sound of the trumpet call!*
>
> *We sing of the uncounted, forgotten by fate,*
> *Tortured in prisons, killed on the block,*
> *They fought for truth, they fought for you,*
> *And fell in heroic, inequitable struggle.*
>
> *Carry your rifles and pistols boldly,*
> *We will strike the bourgeois, we will strike for justice!*
> *An end to shame and base servitude,*
> *We will drown the people's sorrow in blood!*

The Free Combat Druzhina

Shortly after Makhno had returned to Gulai-Polye Marusya proposed a joint action of the Alexandrovsk Federation with the Gulai-Polye A-K Group to seize more weapons. The target was a battalion stationed in Orekhov where the anarchists had enjoyed success earlier. The soldiers in the battalion, part of the 48th Berdyansk Regiment, were about evenly divided between supporters of the Ukrainian Central Rada and sup- Antonov-Ovseyenko
porters of General Kaledin. Again the operation was a success. The regional Bolshevik commander, Bogdanov, was ecstatic about the seizure of arms, which included some mortars. Apparently he assumed that since Marusya was still the deputy of the Alexandrovsk Revkom, the weapons would end up in his hands. Instead all of them went to Gulai-Polye. This incident marked the end of Marusya's loyalty to the Left Bloc authorities. From now on she acted independently.

The commander of the Soviet forces in Ukraine was Vladimir Antonov-Ovseyenko, one of the few Bolsheviks who had attended a military academy. Marusya enjoyed considerable influence with him as she had helped to establish Soviet power in three important Ukrainian cities. He appointed her "commander of a formation of cavalry detachments in steppe Ukraine" and allocated a significant sum of money to her which she used to equip the so-called "Free Combat Druzhina".[19] She was the only woman commander of a large revolutionary force

---

19 Druzhina: another atavistic term referring to the bands of warriors who acted as bodyguards for Slavic princes in the Middle Ages. But the word also implies a group of friends and equals and suggests an internal structure quite different from the armed detachments of the other armed forces in Ukraine.

in Ukraine – an atamansha.

The Free Combat Druzhina was equipped with two large guns and an armoured flatcar. The wagons were loaded with armoured cars, tachankas[20], and horses as well as troops which meant that the detachment was by no means restricted to railway lines. The trains were festooned with banners reading "The Liberation of the Workers is the Affair of the Workers Themselves", "Long Live Anarchy", "Power Breeds Parasites", and "Anarchy is the Mother of Order."

The soldiers were better fed and equipped than many of the Red Army units. Although there were no

Fedor Shuss, anarchist cavalry commander, wearing the typical anarchist "uniform"

official uniforms, the soldiers certainly had a sense of style. Long hair (not common in that era), sheepskin caps, officers' service jackets, red breeches, and ammunition belts were much in evidence. The Druzhina was composed of a core of militants devoted to Marusya and a larger group which came and went on a fairly casual basis. The militants included a fair number of Black Sea sailors, noted for their fighting qualities throughout Ukraine.

With their black flags and cannons, Marusya's echelons resembled pirate ships sailing across the Ukrainian steppe. One observer, the Left-SR I. Z. Steinberg, compared the trains to the Flying Dutchman, liable to appear at any time, anywhere.

Travelling in echelons, the Druzhina advanced to meet the

20 Tachanka: a peasant cart equipped with a machine gun, one of the most devastating weapons of the Civil War in Ukraine.

enemy, which in January, 1918, meant the White Guards and the Ukrainian Central Rada.

The anarchists took part in establishing Soviet power in Crimea. The Druzhina and another anarchist detachment captured the resort city of Yalta and pillaged and the Livadia Palace. Several dozen officers were shot. Marusya next headed for Sevastopol where eight anarchists were languishing in prison. The Bolshevik authorities released the prisoners without waiting for the atamansha. Marusya spent some time in the city of Feodosia where she was elected to the executive of the Peasant Soviet and was able to organize more Black Guards.

The Battles of Yelizavetgrad

On January 28, 1918, the Druzhina appeared in Yeliza-vetgrad, an important city in south-central Ukraine. Its presence allowed the local Bolshevik organization to take over the city Soviet in a bloodless coup, ousting Ukrainian SRs and Kadets[21], and set up their own Revkom.

Soon Marusya was engaged in her usual brand of mayhem. Hearing numerous complaints about the local military commissar, Colonel Vladimirov, she went to his quarters and shot him. Then she organized systematic looting of the city's stores, distributing the goods to the poor. Noticing that people were ending up with things they didn't need, she authorized the bartering of goods although this had been expressly forbidden by the Bolshevik Revkom.

Next Marusya met with the Revkom and sharply criticized its activities. She said its members were "tolerant towards the bourgeoisie". She favoured the merciless expropriation of all property acquired through the labour of others and

21 Kadet: member of the Constitutional Democratic Party, a liberal party which represented the interests of the bourgeoisie in Russian politics.

The railway station in Yelizavetgrad.

a violent response to any attempt at resistance. Belonging to the class of exploiters was a crime in itself, according to Marusya, and she included even the members of the Revkom in this group. She threatened to disperse the Revkom and shoot its chairman for the Druzhina was opposed to any kind of government organ and had not overthrown the Soviet only to have it replaced by another bureaucratic organ.

The Bolshevik administration in the city was extremely troubled by this kind of talk and responded in typical bureaucratic fashion by setting up a special "Committee for the Regulation of Relations with Marusya". This Committee visited Marusya at her headquarters and asked her politely to leave the city, hinting that the Revkom disposed of significant armed forces. Marusya was hardly impressed with this threat, but did leave a few days later after loading up with weapons from a local officers' college after its student body had joined the haidamaks.

On February 9, 1918 a peace treaty was signed between the Ukrainian Central Rada and the Central Powers.[22] The

---

22 Central Powers: the German, Austro-Hungarian, and Ottoman Empires plus Bulgaria.

Central Rada had been losing territory to the armies of the Left Bloc and one of the provisions of the treaty allowed the imperial troops of Germany and Austria-Hungary to establish "order" on Ukrainian soil. German and Austro-Hungarian troops then invaded Ukraine, and, assisted by the haidamaks of the Central Rada, proceeded to push back and mop up the revolutionary forces.

Meanwhile in Yelizavetgrad events unfolded tragically. The city was subjected to the full horrors of civil war. With German forces approaching the city the Bolsheviks hurriedly began to evacuate their troops and institutions, leaving a power vacuum. The day after the Revkom left, a new government called the "Provisional Committee of the Revolution" (VKR) suddenly appeared. Its members were drawn from the parties belonging to the previously overthrown Soviet. Any Bolsheviks remaining in the city were arrested and imprisoned. The new authorities, realizing they would need a military force to protect them from retreating Bolshevik troops, recruited officers who had been in hiding and scoured the countryside for returned military personnel. Peasants were conscripted from nearby villages and their wagons requisitioned. Arms were offered to anyone willing to fight the Left Bloc and its allies.

Unexpectedly the Druzhina returned to the city. Marusya's detachment was at full strength and its arsenal included five armoured cars. At first there were several days of peace between the new civic authorities and the anarchists. The Druzhina took over the railway station and annoyed the citizens mainly by singing anarchist songs. The anarchists sent a truck out every day to collect "contributions" from the bourgeoisie. The Bolshevik prisoners remained in jail.

Then a crisis erupted. There was a robbery at the huge

Elvorta plant – 40,000 rubles were stolen from the payroll office and the workers could not be paid. Wild rumours circulated that the anarchists were responsible and intended to take their revenge on the city for the imprisoned Bolsheviks. Marusya decided to go to the factory herself and explain the situation to the workers which she evidently regarded as a provocation by right-wing elements.

The meeting hall at the plant was filled to overflowing when Marusya arrived (the plant's workforce numbered around 5,000). Leaving her escort at the door, she entered the hall alone and took the stage. But she wasn't allowed to use her oratorical skills – there was ceaseless shouting and cursing. Frustrated at not being allowed to speak, Marusya pulled two revolvers out of her belt and opened fire over the heads of the audience. Panic ensured. Doors were smashed and people jumped through broken windows. Marusya's companions rushed into the hall and rescued her. On the way back to the station her car was fired on and she was slightly wounded.

The alarm was sounded in the city and the new government's militia advanced on the train station. Street fighting went on for several hours. There were many casualties as the anarchists defended themselves with machine guns and grenades. But they were outnumbered many times over by the attackers and Marusya was forced to make a difficult withdrawal to the steppe, stopping at Kanatovo, the first station on the line. At this point Marusya realized that some of her soldiers had been taken prisoner and she resolved to re-engage the enemy to rescue them.

Finally Bolshevik forces arrived from the Front under Alexander Belenkevich, a high ranking officer, and demanded the surrender of the city. His demand being refused, he advanced boldly into the centre of the city where his troops were attacked on all sides. After a three-hour battle, Belenkevich's unit was almost wiped out with many of his troops taken prisoner. Belenkevich himself barely escaped by train. The city authorities began shooting some of the prisoners. Their forces were now led by two retired generals.

Marusya advanced on the city along the railway line from the north but, meeting resistance in the suburbs, she detrained and dug in. The VKR now disposed of thousands of troops under the slogan "Down with Anarchy!" They were armed with both heavy and light artillery, machine guns, and even three airplanes. In order to inflame the population, a story was spread that Marusya looted icons from churches. She was depicted as the leader of a gang of thieves.

A war of attrition went on just outside the city on a front several kilometres long. There was non-stop machine gun and artillery fire. The owner of a distillery, Makeyev, made available unlimited quantities of spirits to the defending troops. To keep up the supply of cannon fodder, the city was scoured for shirkers, who were escorted to the front. There were two lines of trenches: the rear line was manned by officers with machine guns whose job was to block any retreat.

For two days (February 24-25, 1918) the battle see sawed back and forth. On February 26 Marusya received substantial reinforcements in the form of a Red Guard detachment from the city of Kamensk, one thousand workers with a light battery and machine guns. They advanced to the attack with Marusya's troops.

The Red Guards did not fare well in the battle. They lost their artillery and machine guns to the VKR troops and 65 of them were taken prisoner. Meanwhile the artillery of the defenders had the advantage of reconnaissance by airplanes, which also dropped bombs. The anarchist attack got bogged down short of the enemy trenches. They were forced to retreat still further, to the station of Znamenka. There they gained new strength from another detachment under the Left S-R Colonel Muraviev, who had captured Kiev from the Central Rada a few days earlier for the Left Bloc.

The VRK authorities in the city declared for the Central Rada and sent emissaries to the approaching German-Ukrainian forces requesting immediate help. But it was already too late. In battling Marusya north of the city, the VRK had left the south side unprotected. An armoured train known as "Freedom or Death" steamed into the city under the command of the Bolshevik sailor Polypanov. The guard units in the city fled without giving battle. The sailors went directly to the VRK authorities and demanded the release of all prisoners, including Marusya's soldiers. The VRK was forced to comply. The VRK troops north of the city discovered that it was effectively in Bolshevik hands.

Marusya and Muravyev now entered the city. There was more looting and not just by the anarchists. But there were no mass reprisals; in fact Polypanov said at a mass meeting that the three-day battle had been the result of a misunderstanding. The Reds remained in power in Yelizavetgrad until the night of March 19, 1918 when they abandoned the city. Three days later the first German train arrived.

The battles at Yelizavetgrad were typical of the Civil War in Ukraine – desperate encounters between fanatical opponents, with a more powerful third party picking up the spoils. Yelizavetgrad was destined to change hands several more times before the Bolsheviks finally took over.

The Long Retreat

The Left Bloc tried to organize resistance to the German forces in the name of the puppet government they had set up in Kharkov. This was a very unequal contest: comparing numbers alone, the German armies and their allies totaled 400,000 to 600,000 soldiers versus Left Bloc forces of around 30,000, including several thousand in anarchist detachments. Nevertheless there was more than token resistance and the occupation of Ukraine by the Central Powers took up most of the spring of 1918.

The Druzhina stopped in the town of Berezovka in south Ukraine and tried to extort a large sum of money from the inhabitants. Resistance appeared from an unlikely source – a rival anarchist detachment headed by Grigori Kotovsky.[23] Kotovsky had been a real bandit before the Revolution, leading a gang specializing in armed robberies and blackmail. The Revolution had saved him from execution. But now he insisted the

Kotovsky

Berezovkans not give Marusya a single kopeck. Given his superior firepower Marusya was forced to back off.

The Druzhina now detrained and travelled cross-country as a cavalry unit. The detachment made quite an impression as their horses were arranged according to colour: "a row of black, a row of bay, and a row of white – and then again, black, bay, and white. Bringing up the rear were accordionists sitting in tagankas filled with carpets and furs." Marusya herself rode a white horse and many of the troops

---

23 Grigori Ivanovich Kotovsky (1881-1925) was a hero of the Civil War whose reckless adventurism extended well into the Soviet era. He tried to set up a personal satrapy in Bessarabia but his schemes came to an end when both he and his patron, the Soviet military chief Mikhail Frunze, died suddenly under mysterious circumstances.

were dressed entirely
in leather while others
still had their sailor
uniforms. As usual
the Druzhina excited
the envy of the Red
Guards who referred
to it as a "dog's wed-   Tachanka
ding" or even worse names.

A rendezvous for the retreating Red detachments had
been established on a huge estate near the village of
Preobrazhenka. When Marusya arrived she found a Red
Commander, Ivan Matveyev, in charge. Summoned to his
office, she told him she was willing to take orders from
him "until such time as all the detachments have arrived
and it's clear who has the most people."

All she was concerned about, she told Matveyev, was
distributing the goods found on the estate, starting with
clothing. She had already carried out an inventory of the
dresses, jackets, and skirts hanging in the huge wardrobes.
"The property of the pomeshchiks[24]," she said, "doesn't
belong to any particular detachment, but to the people as
a whole. Let the people take what they want."

Mateveyev, visibly annoyed, refused "on principle" to dis-
cuss "rags". Marusya stormed out, slamming the door.

The Bolsheviks decided to disarm the Druzhina before any
more anarchists showed up. They called a general meeting of all the detachments where they intended to seize
the anarchists and disarm them. This was a huge outdoor
gathering in the centre of the estate. Marusya attended
with some, but not all of her troops. The Bolsheviks started
off by talking about the necessity of unity and discipline.
Marusya caught their drift and when one of the speakers

---
24 Pomeshchik: estate owner.

started complaining about the anarchists, she gave a signal for them to leave. When the Bolsheviks finally issued a call to seize the anarchists, they had already slipped away from the estate with their horses and tachankas.

The Druzhina reached a railway line and boarded echelons. Marusya decided to head for her home town, Alexandrovsk, and try to defend it from the German invaders. The city was full of retreating Red Guard detachments. Since Marusya had left a few weeks earlier, relations between the Anarchist Federation and the Bolsheviks had gone downhill. Nevertheless the Bolsheviks were glad to see Marusya because of her reputation as a warrior.

On April 13, 1918, units of the Ukrainian Sich Riflemen broke into the city and captured the railway station. In a warehouse nearby the corpse of a young woman, dressed in leather, was found. A rumour immediately spread through the city that the famous Marusya had been killed. Indeed Marusya took part in the battle, but she was very much alive. A day later the Riflemen were driven out of the city and forced to escape down the Dnieper in boats.

On April 18 the Germans finally entered Alexandrovsk. The Druzhina was one of the last detachments to leave the doomed city. Nevertheless the Bolsheviks accused her of abandoning her positon without permission.

Heading east, the Druzhina stopped at the station of Tsarekonstantinovka where Marusya ran into a disconsolate Nestor Makhno. A nationalist military coup in Gulai-Polye had just resulted in the arrest of the local Revkom and Soviet while Makhno was absent. Marusya proposed a rescue mission but she knew she couldn't accomplish it alone. First she telegraphed the sailor Polypanov but he refused, as did the sailor Stepanov who was also passing through the station with a train packed with refugees. Finally she lined up a Siberian Red Guard detachment led by Petrenko. Marusya still possessed a couple of armoured cars which she proposed to use as spearheads for the attack (Gulai-Polye was eight kilometres from the nearest train station). Just then Marusya received word that the Germans had occupied Pologi, on the line she would need to use to get to Gulai-Polye. She had to abandon her plan and head further east.

Trial in Taganrog

The Bolshevik and anarchists detachments in Left-Bank (Eastern) Ukraine all headed for Taganrog on the Sea of Azov, the current site of the fugitive Ukrainian Soviet government. The Bolsheviks had no hope of hanging on to any part of Ukraine and, so as far as they were concerned, the anarchist troops were no longer necessary. In fact, with their constant agitation against the politics of the party state, they were an ideological liability.

The authorities in the Moscow had already taken steps to get rid of their obnoxious allies. On April 12, 1918 the Moscow Federation of Anarchist Groups was suppressed and almost 400 people arrested. The Bolsheviks propagandized this event as a police action against criminal elements rather than the elimination of political competition. The anarchists in Russia were too weak to counter this action but in Ukraine it was a different story.

Arriving in Taganrog, Marusya found herself accused of leaving the Front (against the Germans) without permission. The task of arresting her and disarming the Druzhina fell to the Red Guard unit commanded by Kaskin. Marusya was arrested at the offices of the Central Executive Committee of Ukraine. As she was being escorted from the building, she noticed the well-known Bolshevik V. Zaton-

sky[25]. She asked him why she was being arrested. When Zatonsky replied, "I
have no idea," Marusya spat at him and
called him a "lying hypocrite".

The disarming of the Druzhina didn't
go smoothly either. The troops refused
to transfer to Kaskin's brigade and demanded to know where Marusya was
being held. The Taganrog Anarchist
Federation and the constantly arriving   Zatonsky
anarchist detachments also demanded that the Bolsheviks
justify their actions. Even the local Left SRs supported the
anarchists.

Contacted by the anarchists, the Bolshevik commander-in-
chief Antonov-Ovseyenko sent a telegram of support: "The
detachment of Maria Nikiforova, and Comrade Nikiforova
herself, are well known to me. Instead of suppressing such
revolutionary formations, we should be creating them."
Telegrams of support were also received from several other Red Guard commanders. And into Taganrog steamed
an armoured train under the command of the anarchist
Garin, a personal friend of Marusya's.

The chief accusation of the Bolsheviks against Marusya
was the pillaging of Yelizavetgrad both before and after
the right-wing uprising there. The other main charge was
deserting the Front, although Kaskin's troops had left the
Front before Marusya's. The anarchists were indignant at
the hypocrisy of the Bolsheviks who used up the strength
of the anarchists in the front lines of the Civil War, while
stabbing them in the back in the rear areas.

A "court of revolutionary honour" was held in late April,
1918. The judicial bench was composed of two local

---

25 Vladmir Petrovich Zatonsky (1888 - 1937), Ukrainian Communist politician, was
executed during Stalin's repressions.

Bolsheviks, two local Left SRs, and two representatives of the Left Bloc government of Ukraine. The Bolsheviks presented a series of witnesses who accused Marusya of crimes which were punishable by death. But there were also many defense witnesses in the packed courtroom, people who disputed the testimony of the prosecution's witnesses and referred to Marusya's services to the Revolution. The anarchist Garin noted that Marusya had faith in the justice of the revolutionary court and added, "If I thought she didn't, my detachment would liberate her by force."

Ultimately Marusya was acquitted of all charges and the Druzhina was given back its weapons. Marusya and Makhno (also present in Taganrog) arranged a series of lectures in the local theatre and various workplaces on the topic: "The defense of the Revolution – against the Austro-German army at the front – against the government authorities in the rear". The pair also issued a leaflet on this topic.

Marusya and Makhno then split up. Makhno and other refugees from Gulai-Polye decided to go home and carry out an underground struggle against the Germans and the Central Rada. Some of the Gulai-Polye people joined the Druzhina. German pressure soon forced the Bolsheviks and anarchists to retreat to Rostov-on-Don. The anarchists collected valuable documents from the local banks – deeds, loan agreements, and bonds – and burned them in a bonfire in the main square. (Cynics noted that paper money was spared.)

An eye-witness described Marusya's crew: "They looked like Spaniards with long hair and black capes.... A pair of large pistols stuck out of their belts, they carried grenades in their pockets. The younger ones wore bell-bottom trousers and gold bracelets... ."

Finally the German advance halted and the long retreat could come to an end. But now the Bolsheviks had reached territory where they had a preponderance in numbers and could safely disarm the anarchists. Marusya saw what was coming and slipped out of the trap. The Druzhina made a dangerous journey north through the Don region, travelling along a railway line partially controlled by White Cossacks, to reach the Russian city of Voronezh where a new front was being formed.

It is difficult to follow Marusya's activities during the next few months. The Druzhina visited a number of Russian towns close to the border with Ukraine. As long as the Germans occupied Ukraine it was impossible for Marusya to carry on above-ground activities in Ukraine.

Finding the Central Rada too radical for their tastes, the German imperialists replaced it with a puppet government under the hetman Skoropadsky. But in November, 1918, the Germans lost the World War. As part of the armistice they were required to evacuate Ukraine. Skoropadsky's government quickly collapsed and was replaced by the Directory, a more radical nationalist group whose leading figure was Simon Petliura. Ukraine was now vulnerable to another Bolshevik invasion as well as to freebooters like Marusya and peasant insurgents like the Makhnovists.

In the fall of 1918, the Druzhina was part of the order of battle of a mixed force which seized Odessa from the Whites who had taken over the city in the power vacuum caused by the withdrawal of the Germans. Marusya then burned down the Odessa prison. This occupation of Odessa was short-lived; the Whites, with backing from Allied troops (French and Greek) were soon back in control.

Trial in Moscow

Marusya next turned up in the Russian city of Saratov, temporary home to many anarchist refugees from Ukraine. There she was arrested by order of the local Soviet and the Druzhina disarmed. During the Red Terror raging at the time (triggered by the attempted assassination of Lenin by an SR), Marusya could well have been shot without trial. Apparently the local Chekists were reluctant to shoot a "heroine of the Revolution" who may have known Lenin in Paris before the Revolution.

Marusya was transferred to Moscow and lodged in Butyrki Prison (where Makhno had spent many years). But soon she was out on bail for she still had friends in high places. The anarchist Karelin and the Bolshevik Antonov-Ovseyenko were prepared to guarantee her good behaviour. Her husband, the Polish anarchist Bzhostek, was also in Moscow. Like many former residents of the Russian Empire with revolutionary credentials, he had been given an important job in the new administration. While awaiting trial, Marusya took the opportunity to enroll in Proletcult, an officially sanctioned movement which encouraged workers to develop their artistic talents.

Marusya was tried in Moscow on January 21–23, 1919 by a court of "revolutionary honour". The Bolsheviks did not refrain from charging her with crimes which she had already been acquitted of in Taganrog, egged on by their exiled Ukrainian puppet government. That government had set up a special commission to investigate her "crimes". According to the chair of this commission, Yuri Piatakov, the Druzhina "disorganized the defense against the Germans and White Guards" and Marusya herself "under the mask of defender of the proletariat kept herself busy with pillaging. She is simply a bandit operating under the flag of Soviet power."

According to the indictment, "M. Nikiforova without the consent of local Soviets carried out in many cities requisitions from quartermaster's stores, private shops and societies; imposed large contributions of money on landowners; and collected guns and other weapons abandoned by the haidamaks. When the Soviets protested, she threatened them, surrounding the buildings of the Soviets with machine guns and arresting members of the executive committees. Her brigade shot a troop commander, and for not carrying out orders she sentenced to be shot the chairman of the Yelizavetgrad Soviet and others."

Her old friend Karelin testified as a character witness, describing her as unselfish: "All she had she gave away even to comrades she barely knew. She wouldn't keep a kopeck for herself. She gave away everything... ." Karelin added she was a complete tee-totaller.

The verdict was published in Pravda on January 25, 1919. Marusya was found guilty of "discrediting Soviet power by her deeds and by the actions of her brigade in several instances; and of insubordination in relation to local Soviets in the sphere of military activities." She was acquitted of pillaging and illegal requisitions.

Marusya could easily have been shot for the crimes of which she was convicted. Nevertheless the court sentenced her "to deprivation of the right to occupy responsible posts for six months from the date of the sentence." The tribunal announced that it had taken into consideration Marusya's services in the struggle for Soviet power and against the Germans.

Return to Gulai-Polye

Although her sentence was light, it seemed onerous to Marusya. Six months was a long time under Civil War conditions. So almost immediately she headed for Gulai-Polye where Makhno had carved out an anarchist enclave by driving out the Whites and Nationalists. Makhno concluded an agreement with the Bolsheviks on February 19, 1919 which allowed him freedom to build an anarchist society. Makhno's short-range plans did not include a confrontation with the Bolsheviks. So he was not particularly happy when Marusya showed up, knowing her bad relations with the Bolsheviks. Makhno made it clear to her that he intended to observe the conditions of her sentence. She was asked to involved herself with kindergartens[26], schools, and hospitals rather than military matters.

An ugly incident occurred at the 2nd Congress of Soviets of Gulai-Polye raion held in the spring of 1919. Marusya, although not a delegate, asked to speak. When she starting attacking the Bolsheviks, the peasants became upset. They were more concerned about the Whites at that point – the Bolsheviks were their allies. Makhno, always a bit of a demagogue when it came to the peasants, physically dragged her down from the podium.

Despite public disagreements, Marusya and Makhno continued to work together. Marusya made trips to Alexandrovsk, nominally under Bolshevik control, which Makhno hoped to include in his sphere of influence. The Bolsheviks responded by arresting anarchists she stayed with, although she was not officially regarded as an enemy of Soviet power.

Gulai-Polye was visited by several high-level Bolshevik

---

26 The anarchist kindergartens were actually known as "children's communes". The Gulai-Polye anarchists were strongly influenced by the Spanish educationalist (and martyr) Francisco Ferrer.

leaders in the spring of 1919, including Antonov-Ovseyenko, Lev Kamenev, and Kliment Voroshilov. Marusya acted as a sort of hostess for these visits and lobbied Kamenev to reduce her sentence from the Moscow court to three months. Apparently she was successful in this.

The visits by the Bolshevik leaders had a sinister purpose: they were trying to figure out when to stop using the Makhnovists for cannon fodder against the Whites and proceed to their liquidation. The Bolsheviks had already suppressed the anarchist organizations in Ukrainian cities under their control. The anarchists were forbidden to hold meetings or lectures, their printshops were shut down, and they were arrested under almost any pretext. This led to an influx of urban anarchists to Gulai-Polye and the territory controlled by the Makhnovists.

Return to Underground Terror

After her sentence had been shortened, Marusya went to the Azov port of Berdyansk in May, 1919, and organized a new detachment using dedicated militants from Makhno's counter-intelligence staff and anarchist refugees from the cities. Among the members of this group was her husband Bzhostek. He had come to Ukraine not to visit his wife but to recruit experienced terrorists for an underground group in Moscow.

Early in June Makhno and his military staff were declared outlaws by the Soviet state. This was an incredibly stressful time for the Ukrainian anarchists. Fighting a losing battle against the Whites in the east, they were now being attacked from the rear by the Bolsheviks. Makhno responded by trying to salvage some military capability. Marusya had other plans.

No longer able to field a regular military force, Marusya decided to launch an underground war against her enemies. But first she needed money. Hearing about Makhno's outlaw status, she and her followers caught up with him at the station of Bolshoi Tokmak. Meeting Makhno in his railway car, she demanded money for her terrorist activities. Makhno cursed and pulled out a revolver. He was too slow – Marusya already had her gun out. After an acrimonious discussion Makhno gave her 250,000 rubles rom his treasury and told her to get lost.

Marusya divided her group into three sections of about 20 each. One group under Cherniak and Gromov was dispatched to Siberia to blow up the headquarters of the White dictator Kolchak[27]. They reached Siberia but were unable to catch up with Kolchak and ended up being absorbed in the anti-White partisan movement.

The second group under Kovalevich and Sobolev went north to Kharkov to free Makhnovist prisoners and blow up the Cheka[28] headquarters. But the prisoners had already been shot and the Chekists had evacuated the city. So the group went on to Moscow to organize a terrorist attack on the Bolshevik leadership. In preparation for this they carried out a number of armed robberies in Moscow and nearby cities top raise funds. On September 25, 1919, they exploded a bomb at a meeting of the Moscow Committee of the Bolshevik Party, killing 12 and wounding 55 prominent party members. In the ensuing manhunt the group was wiped out. After Kovalevich and Sobolev had been killed in shoot-outs, the rest of the group holed up in a dacha and chose to blow themselves up along with a number of Chekists.

---

27 Admiral Kolchak was the leader of the White movement in Russia and aspired to rule the whole country as a dictator. He was executed by the Bolsheviks in February, 1920.

28 Cheka: short for Extraordinary Commission, the original secret police force set up by the Bolsheviks soon after they seized power.

The third group, including Marusya and Bzhostek, headed to Crimea, then under White control, with the intention of blowing up the headquarters of General Denikin, the leader of the White armies in southern Russia. Denikin's headquarters was in Rostov-on-Don at the time but Marusya may have sought help, financial or otherwise, from the Crimean anarchists.

The Last Trial

The last days of Marusya have long been the subject of various legends, resulting from the fact that events in White Crimea were almost impossible for people on "revolutionary soil" to know. The Makhnovists Chudnov and Belash both gave conflicting stories, as did Antonov-Ovseyenko. Only in recent years have documents come to light which clear up the mystery.

On August 11, 1919, Marusya was recognized on the street in Sevastopol and she and her husband were arrested by the Whites. Marusya's group, despairing of being able to rescue her, headed for the Kuban region where they took part in partisan activities in the rear of the Whites.

Marusya's arrest was a great coup for White counter-intelligence and a month was spent gathering evidence for the case against her (difficult under Civil War conditions). Her trial, actually a field court-martial, was held on September 16, 1919 before General Subbotin, commandant of Sevastopol Fortress. The indictment read:

I.   *that the person calling herself Maria Grigor'evna Bzhostek, also known as Marusya Nikiforova, is charged as follows: that during the period 1918-1919, while commanding a detachment of anarcho-communists, she carried out shootings of officers and peaceful inhabitants, and she called for bloody, merciless reprisals against the bourgeoisie and counter-revolutionaries. For example:*

- *in 1918 between the stations of Pereyezdna and Leshchiska by her order several officers were shot, in particular, the officer Grigorenko;*

- *in November 1918 she entered the city of Rostov-on-Don with detachments of anarchists and incited a mob with an appeal to carry out bloody reprisals against the bourgeoisie and counter-revolutionaries;*

- *in December 1918, while commanding an armed detachment, she participated together with the troops of Petliura in the capture of Odessa, after which she took part in burning down the Odessa prison, where the chief warden Pereleshin was killed in the fire;*

- *in June 1919 in the city of Melitopol 26 persons were shot on her order, including a certain Timofei Rozhkov.[29]*

- *These charges involve crimes specified in Articles 108 and 109 of the criminal code of the Volunteer Army.*

II. *Vitol'd Stanislav Bzhostek is charged, not with taking part in the crimes of Part I, but with knowing about them and shielding M. Nikiforova from the authorities.*

Both of the accused were found guilty and sentenced to death. As Part II of the indictment indicates, V. Bzhostek was convicted of the "crime" of being Marusya's husband.

According to reporters at the trial, Marusya was defiant throughout the proceedings and swore at the court after the sentence was read. She only broke down briefly while saying goodbye to her husband. They were both shot.

The newspaper "Alexandrovsk Telegraph" (the city was

---

29 This was an incident which took place on the journey to Crimea.

now in White territory) crowed about her death in its September 20, 1919 issue: "One more pillar of anarchism has been broken, one more idol of blackness has crashed down from its pedestal... . Legends formed around this 'tsaritsa of anarchism'. Several times she was wounded, several times her head was cut off but, like the legendary Hydra, she always grew a new one. She survived and turned up again, ready to spill more blood... . And if now in our uyezd the offspring of the Makhnovshchina, the remnants of this poisonous evil, are still trying to prevent the rebirth of normal society and are straining themselves to rebuild once more the bloody rule of Makhno, this latest blow means we are witnessing the funeral feast at the grave of the Makhnovshchina."

Two weeks after these lines were published the Makhnovist Insurgent Army captured Alexandrovsk from the Whites.

The Legend Continues

Since Marusya had escaped death so many times, it was hard for people to believe she was really gone. Their disbelief created the possibility for false Marusyas to appear. There were at least three of these atamanshas active in the Civil War and they apparently made use of the terror evoked by Marusya's name:

(1) Marusya Chernaya ("Black Maria") commanded a cavalry regiment in the Makhnovist Insurgent Army in 1920-1921. She was killed in battle against the Reds.

(2) Marusya Sokolovskaia, a 25-year old Ukrainian nationalist school teacher, took over her brother's cavalry detachment after he was killed in battle in 1919. She was captured by the Reds and shot.

(3) Marusya Kosova was an atamansha in the Tambov peasant revolt in 1921-1922. After the revolt was suppressed she disappeared from history.

Another legend had Marusya working as a Soviet secret agent. According to this story she was sent to Paris for undercover work and was involved in the assassination of the Ukrainian Nationalist leader Simon Petliura. Petliura was killed by a former member of Kotovsky's anarchist detachment. The only truth in this story might be the fact of anarchists doing the Bolsheviks' work for them.

Maria Nikiforova represents the destructive side of anarchism, the sweeping away of the old to make way for the new. She was not insensitive to the other side of anarchism (see Appendix) but never enjoyed the tranquility necessary to pursue constructive work. Although she had no effect on the ultimate course of the Russian Revolution, she might have for she was always ready to act on her principles at key moments. She devoted her considerable talents to fighting her legions of enemies but eventually fell in this unequal struggle.

The two photographs of Marusya reproduced in this work were probably taken in Yelizavetgrad in 1918. On the back of one of them is written: "Don't think badly of me. – M. Nikiforova".

Appendix

In December 1918 Marusya attended the First All-Russian Congress of Anarchist-Communists in Moscow. The following is the text of a brief speech she gave which was preserved in the minutes:

"Looking at the way anarchists live their lives, I feel depressed at how many deficiencies there are in their work. What is the cause of this? A lack of talent? But that can't be because you can't say there is no talent among the anarchists. But why then are anarchist organizations collapsing? Why, when anarchists followed where their consciences lead them, did they not get those results they had hoped for? For this not to continue, the anarchists must clarify their mistakes.

"In their approach to their work, anarchists must not restrict themselves to the big stuff. Any kind of work is useful. To sacrifice oneself is easier than to work constantly, steadily, achieving definite goals. Such work demands great staying power and a lot of energy. Anarchists don't have enough of this staying power and energy and besides, they must be prepared to submit to comradely discipline and order.

"Anarchists must: 1. be role models (anarchists currently don't have communes); 2. distribute their propaganda widely in printed form; 3. organize themselves and stay in close touch with each other. For this last point we need to register all the anarchists but we need to be selective and encourage not so much those who know theory as those who can put it into practice.

"The process of social revolution is continuing and the anarchists must be prepared for that moment when they must apply all their forces and then each one must carry out their own task, not holding anything back.

"But our work must be based on examples, for example, in Moscow itself we should create a whole network of vegetable gardens on a communist basis. This would be the best means of agitation among the people, people who in essence are natural anarchists."

Bibliography

Primary Sources

Anarkhisti: Dokumenti i Materiali: Vol. 1 (1883-1917), Vol. 2 (1917-1935) (Moscow 1999) [Anarchists: Documents and Materials]

Belash, A. V.; Belash, V. F., *Dorogi Nestora Makhno* (Kiev, 1993) [The Paths of Nestor Makhno]

Makhno, N., *The Russian Revolution in Ukraine (March 1917 - April 1918)* (Edmonton, 2007) [Volume I of Makhno's memoirs]

Makhno, N., *Pod Udarami Kontrrevoliutzii* (Aprel' - Iun' 1918) (Paris, 1936) [Vol. II of Makhno's memoirs: *Under the Blows of the Counterrevolution (April - June 1918)*]

Nestor Makhno: krest'ianskoe dvizhenie na Ukraine. 1918-1921: Dokumenty i materialy (Moscow, 2006) [*Nestor Makhno: the Peasant Movement in Ukraine. 1918-1921: Documents and materials*]

Secondary Sources

Chop, V., *Marusya Nikiforova* (Zaporizhzhia, 1998)

Ermakov, V. D., *Marusya: Portret Anarkhistki*, Sotzial'nie Issledovanniia, No. 3 (1991)

Ermakov, V. D., *Anarkhistskoye Dvizheniye v Rossii: Istoria i Sovremennost'*, (St. Peterburg, 1997) [*The Anarchist Movement in Russia: Yesterday and Today*]

Gody Borby: Istoriko-Revoliutzonnii Cbornik (Zinov'ievsk, 1927) [Years of Struggle: a Historical-Revolutionary Anthology]

Kotliar, Iu. V., *Povstanstvo : Celians'kyi rukh na Pivdni Ukrainy (1917 - 1925)* (Odessa, 2003) [Rebellion: the Peasant Movement in South Ukraine 1917-1925]

Savchenko, V., *Avantiuristy Grazhdanskoi Voiny* (Moscow, 2000) [Adventurers of the Civil War]

Savchenko, V., *Atamany Kazach'evo Voiska* (Moscow 2006) [Atamans of Cossack Troops]

Savchenko, V., *Makhno* (Kharkhov, 2005)

Volkovins'kii, V. M., *Nestor Makhno: Legendi ta Real'nist* (Kiev, 1994) [Nestor Makhno: Legend and Reality]

Fiction

Iu. Ianovski, *Baigorod* (Kiev, 1927)